Stock Market Investing for Beginners:

Stock Market Investing for Beginners as Well as Experts Gives You the Tools to Start Investing Wisely and Successfully. Quickly Cover the Basics Then Learn Actual Actions Steps to Start Trading and Investing Today!

© Copyright 2017 by _____ - All rights reserved.

The follow eBook is reproduced below with the goal of providing information that is as accurate and reliable as possible. Regardless, purchasing this eBook can be seen as consent to the fact that both the publisher and the author of this book are in no way experts on the topics discussed within and that any recommendations or suggestions that are made herein are for entertainment purposes only. Professionals should be consulted as needed prior to undertaking any of the action endorsed herein.

This declaration is deemed fair and valid by both the American Bar Association and the Committee of Publishers Association and is legally binding throughout the United States.

Furthermore, the transmission, duplication or reproduction of any of the following work including specific information will be considered an illegal act irrespective of if it is done electronically or in print. This extends to creating a secondary or tertiary copy of the work or a recorded copy and is only allowed with express written consent from the Publisher. All additional right reserved.

The information in the following pages is broadly considered to be a truthful and accurate account of facts and as such any inattention, use or misuse of the information in question by the reader will render any resulting actions solely under their purview. There are no scenarios in which the publisher or the original author of this work can be in any fashion deemed liable for any hardship or damages that may befall them after undertaking information described herein.

Additionally, the information in the following pages is intended only for informational purposes and should thus be thought of as universal. As befitting its nature, it is presented without assurance regarding its prolonged validity or interim quality. Trademarks that are mentioned are done without written consent and can in no way be considered an endorsement from the trademark holder.

Table of Contents

Introduction 1

Chapter 1: Stock Market Fundamentals 2

Chapter 2: Investor Mindset 8

Chapter 3: Getting Started Buying, Selling and Owning Stocks 12

Chapter 4: Strategies for Success 17

Chapter 5: Stock Market Investing Questions Answered 24

Chapter 6: Building the Perfect Portfolio 27

Conclusion 30

Introduction

Congratulations on downloading *Stock Market Investing for Beginners: Stock Market Investing for Beginners as Well as Experts Gives You the Tools to Start Investing Wisely and Successfully. Quickly Cover the Basics Then Learn Actual Actions Steps to Start Trading and Investing Today* and thank you for doing so. Investing in stocks is a great way to start building real wealth in the long-term but it won't happen overnight. Rather, the most reliable means of doing so will lead to reasonable returns over a prolonged period of time.

Even choosing low-risk investments isn't a sure thing, however, which is why following chapters will discuss everything you need in order to get started investing in the stock market in the right way. First you will learn all about the fundamentals of the stock market and how they can be used for investment purposes. Next you will learn all about the investment mindset and how to train yourself to focus on the long term. From there you will learn how to actually get started when it comes to buying, selling and owning stock. You will then learn numerous different strategies for success as well as the most common questions that those investing in stocks have along with straightforward answers. Finally, you will learn how to create the perfect investment portfolio.

There are plenty of books on this subject on the market, thanks again for choosing this one! Every effort was made to ensure it is full of as much useful information as possible, please enjoy!

Chapter 1: Stock Market Fundamentals

Defining stock: In a most basic sense, one share of stocks represents a partial claim by its owner on the assets and earnings of the company which issued it. The greater the number of total shares on the market, the less that each singular share is worth. Likewise, the more shares of a given company's stock that you own, the greater the control you have over that company. Stock is also referred to as either shares or equity. If you own stock in a company you are referred to as a shareholder which literally means you get a share of the company's profits, which are known as dividends. Dividends are paid out at predetermined points throughout the year. You may also be entitled to voting rights regarding a company's future based on the number of shares of a given company you hold.

While owning shares of a company entitles you to a share of the profits, this does not mean you get an active say in the day to day running of the company, even if you own voting shares. Typically, you will just be able to vote for members of the board of directors during annual shareholder meetings. This way you will be able to indicate your overall pleasure or displeasure at the way the company is currently going.

Understanding risk: When it comes to investing in the stock market, it is important to keep in mind which companies you are considering investing in actually pay out dividends, because not all of them do. What's more, a company that has previously given out dividends is in no way required to continue doing so. This means that there are no guaranteed profits in the stock market as you cannot count on stock appreciation to continuously generate value either. There are dozens of reasons that a given stock can suddenly start to slip, or for the underlying company to go completely bankrupt, potentially even with little or no notice.

While risk is typically thought of as a negative, it should instead be looked at as a tool due to the fact that the greater the amount of risk that a particular stock presents, the greater the potential for reward if it moves in the direction you are hoping for. As such, understanding the right amount of risk for you, which is discussed in a later chapter, is crucial to ensuring you get the ideal rate of return on your investments. When utilized correctly, it is possible to generate greater than the standard 7 percent return that many investments provided and you may be able to squeeze that number has high as 12 percent.

Types of stock
Common stock: There are two primary types of stock that you will come across while looking for investments and common stock, as you may have surmised, is going to be the more frequently seen of the two. Common stock is the type of stock that was discussed above, it provides partial ownership in a company and has the potential to generate dividends as well. Common stock offers a balanced amount of risk and reward, and offers more of both that preferred stock.

Preferred stock: This type of stock provides owners with a related level of ownership in the company in questions, without any of the potential for voting rights. What makes this stock preferred, however, is the fact that it guarantees a set rate of dividends that are guaranteed to be paid out as long as the company is still in business. What's more, preferred stock holders are also paid out for their shares before common stock holders in case the company does go out of business. It's not all positives with preferred stock, however, as the company can buy the stock back, at a premium, at any time without your consent.

Class A and B stock: While there are just the two main types of stock, there are also different subclasses which companies can use if they decide they only want certain individuals to have voting rights. When this occurs, class A stockholders typically get to keep their rights and class B stockholders lose out.

Stock market basics
Each stock is traded on what is known as an exchange with the most well-known being the New York Stock Exchange (NYSE). While previously they were purely physical locations where trading occurred, now they are primarily online destinations with computers making most trades as opposed to actual people. The stock market as a whole exists as a way to ensure securities

exchanges are as simple, easy and risk free as possible. Each stock market can then be broken down into the primary market and the secondary market.

The primary market includes stocks that have just been released to the public, primarily after new companies have had their first initial public offering. The secondary market is where most of the action happens, however, and is the market that most people are talking about when they discuss the stock market in general. It is where individuals buy and sells stocks from one another as opposed to companies directly.

Major markets
US: The Nasdaq and the NYSE are the primary markets in the US. The NYSE is a listed exchange which means that buy and sell orders come throughout at all times during the day as long as the exchange is open. Orders are then matched between buyers and sellers based on the range of prices a buyer is willing to pay for individual shares. If you are looking to buy stock in a major traditional company then you are going to want to check the NYSE first.

While the NYSE still has a physical location that people actually go to, the Nasdaq is purely virtual these days. It is what is known as an over the counter virtual market. While the NYSE is home to many of the largest companies overall, such as Ford and Pepsi, the Nasdaq has traditionally been the home for major technology companies such as Microsoft, Intel and Cisco. If they are working on trading in the Nasdaq, brokerages typically play the role of market maker for the stocks in question.

A market maker is someone who generates a steady string of buy offers (bids) and sell orders (calls) within a range (the spread) that allows them to make a profit on each transaction regardless of the direction the market is moving. While these brokerages typically also match buyers and sellers together, they are also going to hold back a portion of the stock they bring in to ensure that potential investors can always find the trades they are looking for.

Other options: While the US stock markets are some of the largest in the world, they only represent a small fraction of the exchanges available worldwide. Virtually every country has their own stock exchange, though other hubs of note include the Hong Kong Stock Exchange and the London Stock Exchange. Furthermore, there exist what are known as over the counter bulletin boards which typically deal in smaller companies that are not regulated in the traditional fashion. Also known as penny stocks, these types of stocks are broadly considered some of the riskiest investments you can make and are generally not recommended for new traders because the risk typically outweighs the reward.

Market forces
The majority of the stocks that change price in a given day are driven by supply and demand. For example, if a company reports good news then more people are going to want to buy into its stock and the demand, along with the price will increase. If the opposite occurs the amount of supply will increase, decreasing price as a result. While this basic concept is easy to grasp, the reasons why it occurs are much more complicated.

One of the reasons that this is the case is that it can be difficult to determine if specific news is either bad or good. Furthermore, it has to do with the principal theory which states that the cost of a company's stock shouldn't be tied to what a company is worth as disparities appear between these all of the time. As such, the value of a company is typically determined by using what is known as market capitalization which occurs when the current price of the stock is factored into the total number of available shares.

Companies can also be evaluated based on a combination of their earnings and their investors outlook when it comes to future expectations. Earning can be thought of as the sum total of the profit a company made in a specific period of time after expenses have been taken into account. Companies that are listed on the stock market must report their earnings every three months. These reports are then used by analysts to determine an estimate for what the next quarter should look like. If the results match, or exceed, expectations then the stock is likely to rise and if they don't then the stock is likely to decrease in value instead.

The most difficult value to track is public opinion as it doesn't have to necessarily have anything to do with either expectations or results. History is full of times when a given stock did quite well despite never actually generating any true earnings. While investing in stocks when public opinion is on the rise can be extremely profitable, putting it ahead of financial statements is always going to be a risky move because it is bound to come back down to earth eventually.

P/E ratio: This means that when you come across a stock that is currently experiencing a high degree of popularity then your best course of action is going to be looking at its share price along with its earnings per share which is called the P/E ratio. To find this ratio the first thing you will want to do is to take the current value of a given share and divide that be the amount of earnings the company most recently reported broken down to the individual share price. For example, if a company has a share price of $43 and a earning worth per share of $1.95 then its P/E ratio would be 22.05.

This number represents how much you would need to invest in a company in order to see $1 of return based on earnings. In this example, you would need to pay $22 in order to generate $1 of profit. The higher the P/E ratio, the greater the overall level of performance that is expected from the stock by its investors. If you come across a company with a low P/E ratio then it is important to take a look to see if they are currently undervalued, especially if they have recently posted significant profits. If a company has a negative P/E ratio then it will be listed as N/A instead of as a negative number. Obviously, you are going to want to stay away from these companies for investment purposes.

The P/E ratio has a number of limitations that prevent it from being the end-all, be-all of investment advice. First, the ratio for various different industries are typically going to vary dramatically which means it is not a good comparison tool across these lines. Furthermore, the ratio does not account for risk/reward which can lead to inaccurate predictions in some cases. Finally you will also need to keep in mind that publicly traded companies, especially larger ones, have many ways of enhancing the look of their most recent quarter which can lead to false results as well.

Chapter 2: Investor Mindset

Chapter 3 will discuss the importance of making a plan prior to investing in the stock market as well as the specifics when it comes to making your first trade. Making a plan will be useless, however, if you don't work to cultivate the proper mindset for trading prior to getting started, thereby maximizing your effectiveness as much as possible. As such, you are going to want to keep the following tips in mind to ensure your results are as positive as possible.

Stay flexible: The stock market is a volatile place which means that if you ever hope to be successful when investing in it then you are going to need to remain ready to pivot at a moment's notice. The market can change in a matter of minutes which means a stock on a long-running profitability streak can suddenly turn around and become worthless, literally overnight. This means that if you want to succeed you are going to need to limit the influence the past has on your decisions and instead focus on the information available in the present and what it will likely mean for the future. Essentially, you are going to need to be ready to ditch investments that are turning on you and also reevaluate previous choices if you hope to see reliable results in the long term.

Commit to a plan: The plan that you end up creating is going to be critical to your success in the long term, but only if you stick with it every time you choose an investment. While it won't always lead you to success with every trade, if you create it using the proper criteria then it should lead you to make profitable trades greater than 50 percent of the time which means you will win out in the end as long as you stick with it religiously. Furthermore, knowing the acceptable criteria when it comes to selling and buying at a given moment is crucial to ensure that you will be able to take advantage of emerging trends at a time when it will be able to do you the most good.

Have measured expectations: While it is possible to grow rich from investing in the stock market, it is unlikely that this will be a process that happens overnight. Rather, most people who find success there slowly amass assets overtime by holding on to profitable trades and getting rid of those that don't pan out before they can generate too much loss.

Additionally, it is likely to take you a prolonged period of time before you get the hang of things which means you should expect to post a losing record for the first few months you start investing in stocks while you are learning the ropes. It is also important to keep in mind that this is normal and stick with it if you hope to eventually cross from the red into the black. Going into the process with a realistic idea of what it's going to take in order to be successful is an ideal way of ensuring that the learning curve will be as manageable as possible.

Choose personalized strategies: Just because you hear about a strategy that is guaranteed to work because someone else found success with it is no real indicator that it is going to work for you. While there is certainly no reason not to give it a try, it is important to ensure that it stands up to your personal standards and matches your natural investment inclinations as well. If it doesn't it will be unlikely to generate the results you are looking for, no matter how much of a sure thing it is purported to be.

Instead, it is always important to be on the lookout for new strategies that line up with your personal inclinations to use as a stepping stone to stock investing success as opposed to barriers that need to be circumvented in order to see any results. Remaining true to yourself is always going to be most reliable way to see positive results in the long run.

Be disciplined: It is common for many new traders to go after one type of stock or specifics stocks simply because they have a gut feeling about them. The sad truth of the matter is that gut feelings rarely, if ever, pay out effectively. As such, if you follow this scattershot approach you are going to end up making it more difficult to turn a profit in both the short and the long-term. What's worse, if you do end up finding success with this process then all you will be learning is bad habits which will translate to fewer overall successes in the future. Instead of focusing on your gut, it is important to focus on building the discipline you need to make the right choices in the moment even if you gut is telling you something else. While this will likely be hard at first, it will get easier with time.

Seek absolute truth: It doesn't matter if youu feel that the price of a given stock is too low or too high, the only thing you can reliably focus on is the price as it currently stands in the moment. If the facts say that a stock should be valued higher than it currently is then you will want to buy and if it is lower than you will want to sell, end of story. You need to remain impartial about these facts and simply do what they tell you. Developing an attachment to a given stock is only going to hurt your results in the long run.

Focus on logic: After you have formed a successful plan, following it precisely with each trade that you make will always be the most logical choice. This means that even if the trade doesn't end up working out the way you expected, you should still be pleased with yourself as long as you did what made the most sense in the moment. Going off book is only going to lead to failure, far more often than it leads to success. Instead of raging against failed trades, simply look at them as the statistical balance to the other more profitable trades you are likely to make more than 50 percent of the time assuming your plan is sound.

Sometimes doing nothing is the right choice: If you have reason to believe a specific stock is overvalued then you will want to sell, if it is undervalued then you will want to buy. The same principles goes for when a stock is stuck in the middle of the road, in these circumstances then the best course of action is going to be to wait for a stronger signal to appear to indicate a movement in one direction or another. Many new traders find that waiting about without making a move is one of the hardest things to do.

Making trades just to trade is always going to be folly, however, because if the market isn't moving much at all, or if it is moving so much that determining a clear course of action, then waiting for things to normalize is always going to lead to more reliable profits in the long-term. Your goal should always be to make trades for the sake of profit, not just to trade for trading's sake.

Understand that there are no sure things: The odds of finding a system that will accurately predict trades 100 percent of the time, or even 90 percent of the time are extremely small. In fact, you have a better chance of winning the lottery or being struck by lightning than of getting anywhere close to those numbers. There are just too many variables to consider at all times, even before you factor in chance and pure, dumb, luck. Rather than wasting time looking for the impossible, you will find much better results by looking for a plan that you can rely on and just take the additional loss that you will see with a grain of salt.

Chapter 3: Getting Started Buying, Selling and Owning Stocks

When it comes time to prepare to make your fist trade, you are going to need to consider the way you are going to purchase stocks that is right for you and to finalize a trading plan that you can commit to in the long-term. Only by ensuring these things are in order will you be able to get started with the odds in your favor.

Buying stocks
The primary way that most investors go about purchasing stocks is through a brokerage. Brokerages broker deals between buyers and seller while also charging a fee for each trade that is made on top of taking a commission from the results as well. There are two types of brokerages that you will see most frequently, those who offer a variety of services such as trading advice and those that offer a more barebones approach, which are typically online only. Full service brokerages typically have a historical record of successful trading and by using one you will be responsible for less than if you go with an online approach. They are always going to cost you more than online brokerages, however.

It can be difficult to compare various brokerages to one another, simply because it is easy for them to spin their various strengths and weakness in different ways. Nevertheless, you are going to need to persevere as finding the best brokerage for you can easily mean the difference between the success and failure of your stock market investment plans. Specifically, you are going to want to take note of specific fees structures as well as the services that the brokerages offer in order to ensure that you are in the best position to take advantage of what is available to you. Additionally, you are going to want to want to compare margin rates, commissions, word of mouth, account minimums and any promotions they are currently running.

Instead of going through a brokerage, you may be interested in investing in stocks through a dividend reinvestment plan (DRIP) or direct investment plan (DIP). These plans allow shareholders to purchase stock for a given company, from that company directly. To get started with these types of plans you need to purchase shares of a given stock that pays dividends and then reinvest those dividends back into the company in exchange for additional shares.

Preparing a plan
In order to put together a successful trading plan, the first thing you are going to need to consider is what sector of the stock market you want to focus on first. Sticking with one broad category of stocks, at first, is going to make it much easier for you to do your required research. When it comes to choosing the right sector of the market, you are also going to consider how much you have to start investing with, the length of time you are looking to go before making a profit and the type of return on your investment you are hoping for.

With these specifics in mind, you are going to then be able to determine how much risk you are comfortable with taking on in order to see the types of results you are looking for. If you don't like what you come up with, you can either change the amount you hope to generate as profit, the amount of risk you are comfortable with or the amount you have to invest right off the bat. The overall result is always going to be a result of these three factors.

With the results of this metric in mind, you are then going to want to determine which of the strategies in the next chapter are going to be best suited to getting you what you need when it comes to the trades you make. In order to ensure the trades that you make don't head south you are always going to want to go ahead and set stop losses for all of your trades, no matter how much of a sure thing you have reason to believe it might be. A stop loss is a preselected point at which you will sell off your shares if the price moves too low or too high in order to prevent additional losses. The closer a stop loss is to the amount you entered a given trade at, the less you will lose on a high-risk investment.

Furthermore, you are going to need to consider the point where you are going to be willing to walk away from a given trade because you have made enough of a profit from it. Rather than striving to squeeze every cent possible from a given trade, it is important to consider an exit point that finds a balance between profitability and risk. If you find a stock that is proving to be so profitable that you don't want to exit at the predetermined mark, then you can instead sell off half of your holdings at that point and set another exit at a point of greater profit to split the difference between risk and reward.

In order to determine if your plan is successful, the first thing you are going to need to do is give it some time to generate real results. Based on the time frame for profit you determined previously, you are going to want to wait and gather enough data to ensure that you are likely to turn a profit using your plan in the long-term. During this time, you are going to want to take detailed notes including when trades were made, what factors went into your consideration for the trades, the costs and if the trade ended in success. Keep in mind that anything above 50 percent will eventually turn a profit given a lengthy enough timeframe.

Most importantly, if you find a trading plan that works for you, you are going to want to stick with it as diligently as possible, even if your emotions are telling you to go a different way. When trading, your goal should always be to minimize the effect that emotions have on your actions as completely as you can. Trading successfully is all about the numbers which means that emotions are only going to get in the way and almost always end up doing you more harm than good. The more robotically you can execute the trades you are looking for, the greater your profits are going to be across the board. If you find yourself considering making a trade based on emotion, take a moment to ask yourself if you would make the trade if your emotions weren't a factor and then make a choice depending on the answer.

Researching stocks
In order to invest in a stock with confidence, it is important that you research just what exactly you are getting yourself into. This means you are going to want to consider several company documents, outlined below.

10-K: The 10-K form is a form that every publicly traded company needs to file yearly and it outlines everything major the company experienced in the previous 12 months. This should be the first thing you look at as it will give you an overview of the company in question. You will also want to check the 10-Q forms which break down the 10-K into quarterly increments.

Proxy statement: The proxy statement is a public statement that gives you information of the shareholder proposals, board of directors, and management compensation breakdown of a given company.

Annual report: The annual report is a yearly document that includes statements by the higherups in a company to give you a high-level view of where the company has been for the past year and where the top brass think it's going.

Financial statements: For every company you research you are going to want to look up their balance sheet, income statement and cash flow statement as together these three will give you a good financial overview of the company.

Historical Data: While the most recent information on the company is going to be useful, you are also going to want to look into the historical data on the company to determine if where they are at currently is a fluke or if it is the result of years of hard work. This means you will want to take a look at the above documents for the last five years.

Purchasing stock
Once you have done your research, and found a few stocks that fit your plan, you will want to go ahead and actually place your first trade. The execution of a trade can be more complicated than you might expect which is why the following with break down these concepts. First things first, you will want to keep in mind that executing a trade refers to a specific transaction while using the term trade in other contexts can refer to the type of trading plan or strategy you are using.

Based on the current state of the stock in question along with the research you have done, you are either going to want to go long on (buy) or go short on (sell) the stock of the company you have been research. When you place a trade through your brokerage platform, that trade then goes out via their trading network and connects you with another person who is willing to complete the transaction based on the specifications you set. The brokerage you are working with may also have shares of the stock in question available if you are looking to buy. You will then need to pay any relevant fees, plus a commission to the brokerage for the privilege of using their service. It doesn't matter what type of trade you are making, you will also be dealing with the following types of orders.

Market order: This is a request that you send that sets off the transaction that will result in buying or selling. You don't have much control of this request as the market is going to dictate the price you can expect in the transaction.

Limit order: If, based on your research, you like the look of the direction the stock in question is moving you can set a limit order which says you will buy or sell when the price reaches a certain level specifically. This helps to negate the issue of volatility.

Stop order: This is the request to sell off all of your shares of a specific stock if the price hits a precise target. This should be set for every trade at a point just above where holding onto the stock becomes unfavorable.

Stop limit order: This is a combination of the above, and it keeps all aspects of a given stock's movement under close watch for specific triggers.

Trailing stop order: This is more versatile than a standard stop and will only trigger if the price falls to a specific amount of a preset total as opposed to when it reaches a given price. If you are looking to make truly long term investments then these will be your best choice as you can set them based on your overall level of risk assessment.

Chapter 4: Strategies for Success

Price action trading: At its most fundamental, price action trading can be thought of as a way for a trader to determine the current state of the market based on what it currently looks like, not based on what any number of indicators say about it after the fact. This is a great strategy for those who are interested in getting started as quickly as possible as you are only required to study the market in its current form. Additionally, focusing on just the price will make it easier to avoid much of the largely superfluous information that is circling the market causing static which makes it more difficult to determine what is really going on.

In order to determine when to trade using price action, you are going to need to use the trading platform that came with the brokerage you chose and utilize what are known as price bars. Price bars are a representation of price information over a specific period of time broken down into weekly, daily, 1 hour, 30-minute or 5-minute intervals. In order to create an accurate price bar you need the open price for the given stock in the chosen time period, the high for the time period, the low for the time period and the closing price. With this data, you should end up with a box with a line through it. The line represents the high and the low for the day while the edges of the box show the opening and closing prices.

In addition to summarizing the information for the timeframe in question, it also provides relevant information for your purposes. This includes the range of the stock which is a representation of how volatile the market currently is. The bigger the box in relation to the line, the more active the market currently is and the more volatile as well. The more volatile the market currently is, the more risk you undertake when making a specific move.

In addition to the range, you are going to want to consider the physical orientation of the box, if the close price is above the open price then the market improved over the timeframe and if the close is below the open then the market lost value. You are also going to want to take into account the size of the box as a whole. The bigger the box, the stronger the market is overall.

What this type strategy provides you with is a clear idea of what the levels of resistance and support are like for the time period in question. This, in turn, allows you to pick trades with a higher degree of certainty. All you need to do is keep in mind that if demand is stronger than supply then price is going to increase, and vice versa. If the movement indicates that this is likely to continue in the same direction then you will want to pick the point where it is likely to happen again and use that as your entry point. If the opposite is true then you are going to want to sell ASAP to prevent yourself from losing out on gains you have already seen. If the price reaches the support level then demand will exceed supply and if it reaches the resistance level then supply will exceed demand.

Buy and hold: The buy and hold strategy is a type of passive investment in which, as the name implies, shareholders buy into a stock that has strong long-term potential and then hold onto it even when the markets sees a downturn. This strategy looks to the efficient market hypothesis for success which states that it is impossible to see above average returns when adjusting for risk which means it is never a good idea to resort to active trading. It also says that seeing decreases in value in the short term is fine as long as the long-term trend remains positive.

This strategy is very effective when it comes to minimizing the commissions and fees that you have to pay a brokerage because you will only have to do so once before generating an eventual profit. In this strategy, you also don't have to worry about timing the market which is useful for new investors as determining when to buy low and sell high can be much more difficult than it first appears. In practice, the effectiveness of this strategy can vary wildly, depending on when it is acted upon. If an investor first bought stocks in 1960 and held onto them for 50 years then they would have seen nearly a 40 percent return on their investment while someone who bought in starting in 2000 would have since seen a loss of little more than 2 percent if they sold today.

Another major advantage of this type of investment strategy include how easy it is to get started with. All you need to do is research where a number of companies are currently at and consider their future projections to ensure they seem to be moving in the right direction. Once the stock is purchased all you need to do is to check in on your investments from time to time and ensure that nothing catastrophic has gone wrong. Additionally, adopting this strategy means that you will have to pay less in income taxes, specifically capital gains are taxed at a much lower rate in the long term than they are in the short-term.

The disadvantages of this type of strategy include the possibility for nearly unlimited losses because you are not checking in on the stock that frequently, nor watching the markets on a regular basis, you could easily stumble into a situation where the stock in question dropped far enough that it is unlikely that you would ever be able to see enough positive gains again to properly right the ship. With that being said, it is also important that you understand the difference between irretrievable losses and expected decreases as if you panic and make a move when it is not required then you will be stuck with a loss that could have eventually been mitigated when the market righted itself. It is important to have a strong tolerance for risk in order to utilize this strategy for maximum efficiency.

Value investing: This investment strategy is exceedingly simple to understand, though it can be difficult to execute in practice. To successfully value invest all you need to do is seek out companies that are currently trading below their current worth. In order to do so you will want to start by looking for stocks that feature quality fundamentals including cash flow, book value, dividends and earnings. When you find a company that is currently undervalued based on these fundamentals then you are going to want to pounce to take full advantage of the fact before the market corrects itself.

It is important to keep in mind that the key here is to look for value, not junk. This is a crucial difference otherwise you will simply find yourself holding on to stock whose company continue to decline in value. For example, if a company was previously trading at around $25 per share and then drops to $10 per share this doesn't mean that the stock has suddenly become a value bargain. The drop could have been caused by a response in the market that is related to a severe drop in quality of the company in question. In order for it to truly be a bargain it would have to have fundamentals that indicate it is still worth greater than $10 which means the price is likely to increase again instead of continuing to drop.

One of the biggest proponents of this type of investing is Warren Buffet. He held the stock for his holding company Berkshire Hathaway starting in 1967 when it was worth $12 per share and by 2002 it was worth $70,900 per share. While these results are far from average it goes to show how potentially profitable this type of strategy can be if pursued correctly.

The numbers that you are going to want to keep in mind if you hope to invest based on value include the fact that the share price should be no greater than two-thirds of what the stock should be worth based on your research. Additionally, you are going to want to look for companies who have a P/E ratio in the bottom 10 percent of all equity securities. The price/earnings to growth ratio, which is the P/E ratio divided by the growth rate of the company's earnings, should be less than one.

Furthermore, the stock price should never be more than the tangible book value and the company should have less debt than it does equity. The company's current assets should be at least twice that of its current liabilities and its dividend yield should be a minimum of two-thirds of its long-term bond yield. Its earnings growth should be a minimum of 7 percent per annum when compounded for the last 10 years.

Finally, it is important to always factor in a margin of safety as well. A margin of safety is simply a little wiggle room when it comes to potential errors that may have occurred when you were calculating the intrinsic value of the company. To add in a margin of error, all you need to do is subtract 10 percent from the intrinsic value number you came up with.

Growth investing: Whereas value investors are the most concerned with where a company is currently at, growth investors are more focused on the potential future growth of a company to the point of barely considering the current price at all. This investment strategy focuses on buying into companies that are currently trading above their intrinsic value with the belief that this intrinsic value will continue to grow to the point that it exceeds current valuations.

To utilize this strategy effectively you are going to want to primarily keep an eye on young companies as they are traditionally going to grow more rapidly than more established companies. The theory behind this strategy's success is that this growth in revenue or earnings will then directly translate to an increase in the underlying stock price. Other common investments include companies in rapidly expanding industries, frequently those that are related to new technologies. Profits are then realized not through dividends but through capital gains as it is uncommon for growth companies to pay dividends as they typically reinvest the money that would be going to dividends directly back into the company instead.

Unlike most of the other strategies discussed here, there are no hard and fast guidelines when it comes to investing in growth companies. However, tthere are certain criteria which can be used as a framework for your analysis those these must be applied to each company with an eye towards a company's unique situation. Some of the things you will want to keep in mind include the current state of the company in relation to its past performance, and its performance compared to its industry as a whole.

It is also important to consider if the company has been growing based on its annual revenue for the past five years. If the company is currently worth more than 4 billion dollars then you would want minimum growth to be at least 5 percent. If the company is worth between 400 million and 4 billion dollars then you would want the minimum growth to be at least 7 percent. If the company is currently worth less than 400 million dollars then you would want to see a minimum to be at least 12 percent growth.

Additionally, you will want to consider the company's forward earning growth with a project growth rate of anywhere between 10 and 12 percent typically being enough to pull the trigger, though 15 percent is even better. It is important to keep in mind that these are just estimates, however, and estimates can always change.

Finally, you are going to want to determine if the stock is likely to double within the next five years. If not, then it is likely not a growth stock. While this might seem like a high standard, if the projected growth rate is 10 percent then it will double in value in seven years which isn't that much longer.

Growth at reasonable price (GARP) investing: The GARP method of investing is a combination of both growth and value investing. It looks for companies that are currently slightly undervalued and also has a sustainable growth potential. It typically looks for stocks that are currently somewhat less undervalued than those that value investing looks for while expecting slightly less from the stocks it chooses than growth investing.

Much like growth investing, GARP investing is concerned with the growth of a prospective company. When using this method you are going to want to see positive earnings from the past few years as well as positive earnings projections for the coming years. Unlike with growth investing, however, the ideal range of growth in the next five years is going to be between 25 and 50 percent instead of 100 percent. The theory here is that higher growth rates lead to high rates of risk.

GARP investing is also going to share metrics for potential companies with growth investing, though the ideal levels are going to be lower. A good company to invest in with the GARP method is going to see positive cash flow and positive earnings momentum. Outside of that, however, you are going to have some more freedom when it comes to choosing the best companies when using this strategy as subjectivity is an inherent part of GARP investing. Regardless of the specifics it is important to always analyze companies in relation to their unique contexts as there is no ideal formula for what makes a good GARP investment.

It is also important to be on the lookout for P/E ratios that exceed those which are preferred in value investing, while also ensuring that they are lower than those preferred in growth investing. While a growth investor will look for P/E ratios of between 50 or 60 times earnings, GARP investing looks for something in the 15 to 25 times range, trading the excess profit for more reliability.

The PEG ratio is typically considered the most important GARP investing metric because it essentially gauges the balance between value and potential growth. GARP investing requires companies to have a PEG that is no higher than 1 and ideally around the .5 range. A PEG in this range implies that currently, the price of the stock is lower than it should be to some extent based on the company's current earnings growth. If you come across a stock in this range then it is a strong indication that, at the very least, it requires additional analysis as you may be on to something.

Chapter 5: Stock Market Investing Questions Answered

Is there evidence I will make money buying stocks?
Based on data acquired from Standard and Poors, the average return from stocks between 1926 and 2013 was 9.9 percent. While this means you can certainly make money investing in stocks, it doesn't take into account the risk for doing so. There are no guarantees that the stocks you pick will end up providing a return on your investment, especially as a new investor who has yet to learn the ropes. Risk leads to the greater potential for reward, however, so if you create a reliable plan and stick with it you are more likely to come out ahead in the long run.

What are the best ways to tell if a stock is healthy?
While the exact metrics that will tell you if you should invest in a stock are going to vary based on the stock investing strategy you choose, you are always going to want to start by looking at the quarterly earnings report every publicly traded company is required to submit to the Securities and Exchange Commission (SEC). Primarily, you are going to want to look into the P/E ratio, the earnings per share and the price/book ratio which shows what shareholders are willing to pay compared to the reported value of the company.

How do I find analyst recommendations related to a particular stock?
While it is important to do your own research based on the trading strategy you have chosen, you will still want to see what the professionals have to say, especially when you are first starting out. Research from respected analysts can be found online via resources such as Finance.Yahoo.com, Zacks.com and MorningStar.com. Likewise, if you are using a full-service brokerage firm they often provide analyst recommendations as well. Additionally, Zacks.com provides a record of various analyst's success rates.

How can I buy into an IPO?
Many IPOs are not open to the masses and are reserved for serious investors only. To determine if a specific IPO is open to

you, you will want to seek out the company's SEC registration and look in the section on underwriting. This will provide you with details regarding the financial institutions who are involved in the IPO in question. You can then take that information and use it to find a broker that is affiliated with one of those institutions and ask them about the IPO directly.

What does shorting stock mean?
When an investor shorts a stock, what essentially happens is that they more or less borrow the stock from the brokerage and sell it to another buyer because they feel the current price is overvalued. Assuming the price then drops, the investor who shorted it makes money on the difference it sold for and what they have to pay for it after the price has dropped. Shorting stock is only possible if your brokerage allows you to trade on margin which means you are able to trade with more money than you actually have in your trading account.

What is a reasonable return for a novice investor?
Since the early 1900s, the stock market has seen an average rate of return of about 10 percent. With inflation taken into account, this means you could see your investment double in about 10 years. This doesn't mean you are always earning 10 percent per year, however, because it is an average. However, this amount is hotly contested by financial experts. Conservatively the rate you can expect is generally considered to be between 7 and 8 percent.

Should I put money into a hedge fund?
Hedge funds typically invest in more than just stocks, and some of these investments are not regulated by the SEC which makes it difficult to determine what their value is or to ensure their liquidity. Furthermore, they are generally only an option for what are known as accredited investors which are those with a net worth that is more than one million dollars at the time they buy in to the fund or those that make more than 200,000 dollars per year. All told, they are not a good choice for novice investors.

Should I buy into an exchange-traded fund (ETF)?
Exchange-traded funds have the flexibility of stocks and the low costs of mutual funds. Unlike mutual funds, however, they focus primarily on stock indexes. This means their price is always changing and you have the option to sell at any time. As there are many different types of ETFs it is important that you understand the ETF you are considering, its goals and how they match up with your personal financial objectives. If you have a large IRA that is going to roll over or if you have a large amount of money to invest then an ETF can be a good choice, otherwise you are likely going to want to consider other options.

Why do companies issue shares?
Companies issue shares of stock in order to receive an influx of capital. The amount of capital that they receive is going to vary based on the number of shares they issue and how much each of their shares are valued at. In turn, the company then uses this cash to grow their business without having to worry paying back the money as they would with a loan. If the company is successful they can they buy back their shares or issue more to take advantage of their success.

How are stocks taxed?
Capital gains on stock investments can be taxed at up to 15 percent if you hold onto a given stock for more than one year. If you sell the stock in less time than that any profit that you make is instead considered a short-term gain and, as such, is taxed the way any of your other income is. Dividends are typically taxed at 15 percent as well if you hold them for a specific period of time after the last dividend was paid out which is typically about two months.

Chapter 6: Building the Perfect Portfolio

The following is an outline that will help you set up an investment portfolio that you don't have to micromanage. If done properly it is a great way to build wealth for the long term with relatively little effort. If you have a 401(k) plan that is sponsored by your employer then you can link that to the investment account that you will need to set up for use with your portfolio, if you don't have a 401(k) then you'll need to open a fresh investment account instead. Ideally you will want to use an individual retirement account (IRA) as this will ensure you have to pay the minimum amount of taxes possible, in exchange for not being able to remove funds without penalty until you are ready to retire.

Doing so is as easy as doing research on various investment firms that offer IRAs such as Fidelity or Vanguard, you will also want to look into bank sponsored investment IRA accounts such as those offered by Wells Fargo. If you have a 401(k) then you will need to ensure that it rolls over properly. You will also need to connect your investment account to a savings or checking account in order to purchase index funds or bonds.

Determine your asset allocation: While you will want your portfolio to be largely comprised of stocks, the best portfolios include a variety of different investments. At a minimum, you are going to want to allocate some funds to bonds in addition to stocks. The amount you allocate to each type is going to vary based on your investment goals, risk tolerance and age. A general rule of thumb is you start with the number 110 and subtract your age from it. That is the percentage of your portfolio that should be in stocks. For example, if you are 30 then you should put about 80 percent of your funds into stocks. As you age you are going to want to move a larger percentage to low-risk investments.

Consider index funds: Index funds are a collection of bonds or stocks that work to mirror specific sections of the market, they typically offer low fees and average returns that are on par with what you can expect from stocks or bonds on their own. The best funds to pick are those that offer minimum risk in exchange for moderate returns. One of the most popular is the Vanguard Total Bond Market Index Fund. You may also want to consider a stock market index fund which is a mix of international and local stocks. This way you will avoid scenarios where a significant drop in the value of stocks in one are causes you to lose your entire investment in one fell swoop.

When considering various funds, you are going to want to keep in mind that some have minimum buy-ins or other conditions. Do some research before deciding on the best one for you, just because your portfolio is going to be set up to maximize profit while minimizing the work you need to do doesn't mean you should be lax when it comes to setting up the specifics. Additionally, you will want to keep in mind that often if you buy into a fund more substantially later on you will often see better rates.

When looking into your options it is important to keep in mind any limitations that are placed on you by your 401(k). Some 401(k)s limit the funds you have access to, be sure to do your research on each before choosing as they are likely to vary dramatically. Even if the end result isn't as robust as the funds that are available on the open market, it is worth sticking with your 401(k) in order to take advantage of its superior tax benefits.

Contribute to the fund on a regular basis and rebalance about once per year: Once you have determined the funds you are interested in buying into and the asset allocation you are going to start with, the next thing you will want to do is to set up an automatically reoccurring deposit to be added to your portfolio on a regular basis. It doesn't matter if the amount is small, when taken over a large enough timeframe, even an extra two-hundred dollars per month is going to add up. If you have a 401(k) this is extra important as it means that the money will be tax-deferred. As long as you treat your investments like you would any other bill you will never be tempted to tap into those funds for other purposes.

With that done, you will then essentially want to forget about your portfolio until it comes time to readjust your metrics. You may want to switch from international and local stocks to a balance of local stocks in different industries or increase the amount you are putting into bonds. Whatever it is, you are only going to want to do so about once per year, at most. When you rebalance, you will want the total asset allocation to remain the same as when you started, at the very least. Be aware that if you change stocks you will have to account for additional fees.

Consider a target-date fund: If you are looking for the absolute simplest portfolio option then you may want to consider a target-date fund. These types of funds do all the work for you, they split your money up in a balanced way to covers bonds, stocks and additional holdings all you have to do is provide them with a date for when you want to start taking advantage of the money you have earned. It even adjusts these ratios over time to assure that you have the right mix of allocations based on your age. The only other thing you will need to provide is your tolerance for risk. The only real downside to a target-date fund is the fact that the fees will be higher than with other types of funds.

Conclusion

Thank you for making it through to the end of *Stock Market Investing for Beginners: Stock Market Investing for Beginners as Well as Experts Gives You the Tools to Start Investing Wisely and Successfully. Quickly Cover the Basics Then Learn Actual Actions Steps to Start Trading and Investing Today*, let's hope it was informative and able to provide you with all of the tools you need to achieve your goals, whatever it is that they may be. Just because you've finished this book doesn't mean there is nothing left to learn on the topic, expanding your horizons is the only way to find the mastery you seek. When it comes to investing in the stock market it is important that you continue seeking out new information as the market is always changing, if you rest on your laurels you may find that your surefire plan is suddenly less effective than it previously was.

Now that you have finished reading it is time to stop reading already and to get ready to get started investing in stocks. The potential for serious profit definitely exists but only if you are willing to give your investment plan the time it needs to start generating a profit in a serious way. This means developing a plan that works for you and sticking with it through the good times and the bad.

Don't forget, no plan is ever going to be 100 percent successful, no matter how much research you do or planning you put into it. Investing in stocks is a numbers game and if you try and change your plan every time something goes array you will skew the numbers, and not in your favor. Remember, investing in stocks is a marathon, not a sprint, slow and steady wins the race.

Finally, if you found this book useful in anyway, a review on Amazon is always appreciated!

Description

If you are looking for a way to save for retirement that is more effective than simply socking money away in a savings, account, there are few more effective ways of doing so than via the stock market. If you are interested in learning how to make the market work for you, then *Stock Market Investing for Beginners: Stock Market Investing for Beginners as Well as Experts Gives You the Tools to Start Investing Wisely and Successfully. Quickly Cover the Basics Then Learn Actual Actions Steps to Start Trading and Investing Today* is the book that you have been waiting for.

Since the early 1900s, the stock market has seen an average rate of return of about 10 percent which is higher than just about any other type of investment return. With inflation taken into account, this means you could see your investment double in about 10 years. It isn't a surefire system, of course, but with great risk comes the potential for great reward and with the tools found inside you will be able to minimize the potential risk while maximizing the potential for reward. This includes things like the ideal investor mindset, the top five strategies for stock market investment success and a step by step guide designed to get you investing as quickly and effectively as possible.

So, what are you waiting for? Stop crippling your savings by letting them languish in a savings account and start putting them to work in a big way. Take control of your financial future and buy this book today!

Inside you will find
- Everything you need to know about the stock market to start investing with confidence right away.
- The secret to developing the mental fortitude to start investing effectively.
- A step by step guide to preparing a personalized investment plan that really works.
- A detailed breakdown of price action trading, value investing, growth investing, GARP investing and buy and

hold investing and how each can work to make you money.
- The easiest way to put together an investment portfolio that generates maximum returns and minimal headaches.
- ***And more...***

Property Investing:

How to Create Wealth and Passive Income Through Smart Buy & Hold Real Estate Investing. An Exact 18-Month Strategy for Making an Extra 100k Per Year

© Copyright 2017 by _____ - All rights reserved.

The follow eBook is reproduced below with the goal of providing information that is as accurate and reliable as possible. Regardless, purchasing this eBook can be seen as consent to the fact that both the publisher and the author of this book are in no way experts on the topics discussed within and that any recommendations or suggestions that are made herein are for entertainment purposes only. Professionals should be consulted as needed prior to undertaking any of the action endorsed herein.

This declaration is deemed fair and valid by both the American Bar Association and the Committee of Publishers Association and is legally binding throughout the United States.

Furthermore, the transmission, duplication or reproduction of any of the following work including specific information will be considered an illegal act irrespective of if it is done electronically or in print. This extends to creating a secondary or tertiary copy of the work or a recorded copy and is only allowed with express written consent from the Publisher. All additional right reserved.

The information in the following pages is broadly considered to be a truthful and accurate account of facts and as such any inattention, use or misuse of the information in question by the reader will render any resulting actions solely under their purview. There are no scenarios in which the publisher or the original author of this work can be in any fashion deemed liable for any hardship or damages that may befall them after undertaking information described herein.

Additionally, the information in the following pages is intended only for informational purposes and should thus be thought of as universal. As befitting its nature, it is presented without assurance regarding its prolonged validity or interim quality. Trademarks that are mentioned are done without written consent and can in no way be considered an endorsement from the trademark holder.

Table of Contents

Introduction 37

Chapter 1: Property Investment Mindset 38

Chapter 2: Finding the Money 41

Chapter 3: Mistakes to Avoid 47

Chapter 4: Getting Started with Your 18-month Strategy 51

Chapter 5: Flipping Properties 55

Chapter 6: Rental Properties 60

Conclusion 66

Introduction

Congratulations on downloading *Property Investing: How to Create Wealth and Passive Income Through Smart Buy & Hold Real Estate Investing. An Exact 18-Month Strategy for Making an Extra 100k Per Year* and thank you for doing so. Real estate investment is one of the oldest and most reliable forms of investment in the world and if you follow the plan outlined in the following chapters you can start seeing real results in just a year and a half.

This doesn't mean that doing so will be easy, however which is why the following chapters will discuss everything you need to do in order to get into the real estate game successfully and also see real results from doing so. First you will learn about the true real estate investor mindset. Then you will learn about the ways you can find money to fund your real estate investment dreams without having to pony up the full cost yourself. From there you will learn about real estate investment mistakes to avoid on your journey to financial freedom. Next you will learn what you need to get started on your 18-month journey before finally learning how to go about making a profit from flipping houses and then using those profits to ultimately generate long-term income through investing in rental properties.

There are plenty of books on this subject on the market, thanks again for choosing this one! Every effort was made to ensure it is full of as much useful information as possible, please enjoy!

Chapter 1: Property Investment Mindset

In order to invest in real estate successfully, especially if you hope to make $100,000 in the next 18 months, you need to have a mindset that is primed for success. That means you need to cultivate the following suggestions into your daily life. Don't try to incorporate them, make a concentrated effort to do whatever needs to be done to ensure you build your investment mindset in the right way, starting right now.

Have the right perspective: First things first, it is important to develop a long-term perspective when it comes to investing in real estate successfully. Sure, if you follow the plan outlined in this book, you stand a good chance of making $100,000 in the first 18 months, but you are also going to want to look beyond this timeline if you hope to truly be successful in the real estate investment industry. Likewise, it is important to keep in mind that something is likely going to come along and shake up your plan every few months. The way you deal with these upsets is going to go a long way to determining what kind of real estate investor you really are. Don't let them shake your commitment, remain committed to the cause and will yourself to find the success you seek.

Be disciplined: In order to reach your initial goal in just 18 months, you are going to need to work while other people are playing and delay thoughts of gratification until your new venture is all the way up and running. While this is easy to say, many people find it much more difficult to commit to in practice. As such, you will find that you are more successful at it when it counts if you don't wait until the rubber hits the road to start practicing. Live every day in a self-disciplined manner and you will find it much easier to keep up the good work when it matters most.

Keep your goals in mind: If you hope to find success in just 18-months then you are going to need to remain focused on that fact every hour of every day. When the going gets tough, let your dedication to your goal be enough to keep you motivated and keep you moving forward. When things fall apart due to unforeseen circumstances, don't focus on the negatives and instead just keep moving forward. As long as you keep your goal in mind you will find that everything else that gets in your way is little more than an easily avoidable distraction between you and true success.

Don't be afraid of hard work: The average millionaire works sixty hours per week. In order to meet your goal in the next 18-months you are likely going to need to spend forty hours per week working to survive and nearly that many preparing your investment strategy, hiring a team, finding a way to pay for it, finding properties and ensuring they are ready to be sold or rented when the time comes. Don't waste your work time, make every hour count.

Follow through on your plan: This book outlines the steps you need to take in order to ensure you make $100,000 per year in real estate investing starting with an 18-month period of preparation. In order to do so you are going to need to prioritize the activities in the right way and focus on completing them in the correct order to maximize your effectiveness. Each day you should make a point of considering what the best use of your time is at any given point and then doing everything you can to follow through on that action.

Never stop learning: There are always new and improved ways for finding new properties and maximizing the value of the properties that you do own coming into existence. Resting on your laurels, even after the first 18 months is only going to lead to decreasing returns over time. Even once you hit your goal, you can still do better, make it a point of studying real estate for at least an hour per day while you are getting started, and then at least an hour per week when you are on your way. Listen to podcasts about it, read books, take classes and seminars, immersing yourself in the topic will only lead to greater success in the long run.

Remove failure from your vocabulary: Seventy percent of people who attempt to invest in real estate in the way you are attempting to fail to achieve their goals for one reason or another. This doesn't matter however, because you aren't going to be one of them. Strive to develop a positive mindset and don't let anything get between you and your belief in success. Failing and persevering will only make you stronger, it is the fear of failure that is likely to hold you back. Take calculated risks towards achieving your goals and never be afraid of following through on them just because success is not guaranteed.

Look for the right opportunities: Those with a successful real estate investment mindset don't approach opportunities by thinking about what it will cost them, they consider what the opportunity could net them assuming it works out correctly. Thinking about things in terms of cost helps to create a limiting mindset, thinking about them in terms of the value they provide will allow you focus your time, energy and money towards the things that will do the most good the greatest percentage of the time.

If the benefits are worth the price, then you should be willing to go for it, no matter what that price is. There is always a way to find the money for a profitable venture, regardless of whether you have it in your pocket right now. It is important to not let a lack of immediate funds slow you down when it comes to hitting your goals. Instead of focusing on what you don't have, spend that energy considering the various ways you can crunch the numbers, work the system and take as full advantage of the opportunity as you possibly can.

Chapter 2: Finding the Money

One of the many difficult things about getting started in real estate, assuming you don't have $100,000 plus sitting around, is finding the right way to pay for your initial investment in a way that makes the most sense for you. Luckily, there are numerous different options to choose from in order to get someone else to bear the brunt of the upfront costs. Before you start looking in earnest, however, it is crucial that you do some homework up front in order to know exactly what you are getting into.

Borrowing from a position of strength
In order to ensure you get the best deal on your loan as possible, it is important to know what tools you have at your disposal when it comes to finding the right type of financing. To get started, you are going to want to check your credit report and seek professional help if your score isn't where you want it to be. Unfortunately, a high credit score isn't all that is required these days as the Great Recession has made it much more difficult to finance an investment property than it once was. This means you will naturally start at a disadvantage if you don't have an extensive credit history or lots of previous investment experience. Difficult is a long way from impossible, however, as long as you approach lenders with the following:

Significant down payment: Currently most traditional lenders are going to require that you have at least 20 percent of the total cost of the investment you are requesting financing for in hand before they will give the go ahead. If you are considering hard money lenders (discussed in detail later in this chapter) then you will likely need 40 percent instead. However, if you can put down an extra 5 percent then you will likely start to see a significant decrease in rates almost immediately. Being able to offer up a larger down payment will also make it more likely that financial institutions will be more forgiving when it comes to overlooking less than perfect credit; this will only take you so far, however.

If you don't have the full 20 percent down payment for the property you are considering, but you qualify for a bank loan in all other respects, then you may want to consider getting two loans rather than just one, just keep in mind that it is going to cut into your profits substantially and it can be more difficult than getting just one mortgage as well. If you do pursue this course of action, however, it is important that you strive to pay off one of the mortgages as quickly as possible to cut down on the interest you will pay.

Have the right credit rating: Once you know your credit rating you will be able to more readily determine what type of loan you can expect to find and what the interest rates are likely to be. Anything that is below 740 is going to cost you in terms of interest rates and monthly payments and interest rate hikes. In general, this typically works out to about 2 additional points of interest for every 10 points your credit score drops. If you are looking for a lower payment amount then you will have a higher amount of interest and vice versa.

Furthermore, prior to going to see any lenders you are going to want to gather up a list of all of your investment and personal expenses for the previous six months along with proof that you can afford them plus the additional expenses that the loan will add to your plate.

Ask the right lenders: If you don't meet, or even better exceed, the minimum requirements for the larger financial institutions then you will likely be better off looking into alternatives rather than taking the less favorable loan these lenders will give. The best place to start is going to be local credit unions as their requirements are typically laxer than the major players, especially if your property is in their area. These lenders often have a strong interest in seeing their local area prosper which means they will be more likely to look the other way on things that would be deal breakers with larger lenders.

Another viable choice these days is to ask for owner financing. Prior to the Great Recession, when virtually anyone with a pulse could get a bank loan, asking for owner financing was a turnoff to potential sellers because it meant your credit was absolutely in the pits. This perception has changed, however, and now approximately 20 percent of all sellers are willing to consider the idea at the very least. If you do obtain owner financing you will then sign a promissory note that outlines the specifics of the agreement including how long it will take you to pay back the loan and what the interest rate is going to be.

Other lender options

Long-term considerations: As you are not looking to purchase just one investment properly, but looking to make this a regular occurrence, you are going to want to put in the time upfront to find a lender that you are comfortable building a long-term relationship with. While it will require extra work up front, this relationship will ultimately make it easier to complete the loan process in the future. You will be able to work together to form a strategy that will help to ensure that everyone comes out on top in the long run. You will want to be wary of taking a loan from a real estate broker, however, as they are going to be much pickier about the types of properties you are free to purchase.

You will also need to keep in mind that the lender is going to directly distributing your loans which means you are going to want to interview them before you sign anything. You should always ask every lender the following questions:
- How many investors total are you currently working with?
- What is the maximum number of loans you allow individual investors to have active at a single time?
- Are there some types of real estate investments you typically favor over others?

These questions will then make it easier for you to confidently choose the right lender for you based not on a sales pitch but on cold hard facts. It will also allow you to alter your pitch based on what you've learned, if appropriate. If you don't like the answers you receive, you will then be able to move on and keep from wasting your time either waiting to be preapproved for a loan or from being given rates that you aren't going to be able to profit from.

Hard money loans: If you are looking for an alternative to traditional lenders, or simply don't have the credit to qualify for one of their loans, then a hard money loan might be a good choice. A hard money loan is a loan that is provided by a private investor instead of a bank or a credit union. These loans will generally be for shorter periods of time and the majority of the payments you will make will go towards interest with a large balloon payment coming at the end of the cycle to square up on the principal of the loan.

Hard money loans are frequently appealing to new real estate investors due to the fact that the lender is going to be more interested in the quality of the proffered investment opportunity than if you have successfully invested in real estate before. When it comes to determining the right hard money lender to use, the best place to start looking is at your local real estate investment club. In general, when it comes to finding out details on investment in your area, then a real estate investment club is a great place to start as you will almost always find someone who can show you the ropes.

Finding a local club should be as easy as getting online and doing a little research and even mid-sized towns are likely to have one or two meeting somewhere on a regular basis. Even if you don't end up getting a loan through the connections you make there it will still likely pay off in one way or another down the line as there are plenty of things these folks can teach you.

When looking into different hard money lenders you are going to want to keep in mind that they typically focus on different types of real estate deals. Most hard money lenders operate via what is known as first lien position. This means they are going to be the first ones to get their money back if you end up selling the property off early due to unforeseen circumstances. Second lien position hard money lenders, those who would get their money back after your initial investment was recouped, can be found, though they are much rarer.

The interest rates you will be able to find when it comes to hard money loans are generally going to vary based on your location as well as the number of other hard money lenders in the area.

In general, however, the amount is always going to be higher than what a bank is going to charge and will typically be in the 10 to 15 percent range with the specifics of your investment and your personal finances going a long way to move the average a few points one way or another. Additionally, points will range between 2 and 4 percent on the amount of the loan.

The total amount that a hard money lender will be willing to put forth will be based on what is known as the loan to value ratio. This ratio can be found by taking the value of the potential loan and then dividing that number by the total value of the loan and dividing it by the total estimated value of the property you are trying to purchase once it has been completely renovated. In general, a hard money lender will be willing to give you anywhere from 65 to 75 percent of the value of the property in question.

It is also possible to find hard money lenders who will pay almost the full amount required or even chip in for the costs of the renovations. These are a much riskier proposition though which means they will expect as much as 20 percent of the total profits when things are said and done. If you are looking to get started with little or no money down then it can be worth the decrease in overall profit.

When approaching a hard money lender, you are going to be sure that you really have all your ducks in a row in order to do your best to guarantee your success. As such, you will want to have a credit score that is at least 600 along with an income debt ratio below 45 percent and a credit history that has been clean from foreclosures or bankruptcies for at least 10 years. You will also need to show that you can afford all of your expenses plus the payments that would be required. Finally, you will need to show that you will have equity invested in the property that will function as collateral to ensure you will pay back the loan as opposed to vanishing into the night.

Alternately, you may want to consider alternatives to investment loans, especially if you are looking to put down as little as possible up front. Title loans, equity loans based on other property you own or even credit cards can all help you to get started though they should only be used as a last resort because the rates and payments are always going to be much higher than even slightly more conventional options.

Chapter 3: Mistakes to Avoid

As a new investor in the real estate market, you will likely find that every move you consider making fills you with anxiety, simply each and every action has the potential to affect you so greatly for good or for ill. This is a natural part of the learning process, however, and learning while doing is naturally going to lead to some mistakes now and then. While you will want to view any potential mistakes as learning experiences, there are some that you definitely don't want to experience for yourself. Keep the following in mind and avoid these major new investor pitfalls at all costs.

Planning at the viewing: If you find yourself looking at a potential property without first having a clear plan for utilizing it effectively already in mind then you are already starting off at a huge disadvantage when it comes to deciding the right amount to offer for the property. If you don't already know everything about the property beforehand then it will be much more difficult to make an offer that is sure to make you as much money as possible from it. When working towards your 18-month plan, you are going to have very little wiggle room when it comes to getting everything just right, which means knowing your numbers is a must if you want to stay on track.

Many new investors fall into the business by initially purchasing a property for a price that they feel is simply too good to pass up. They then find themselves with property in hand and no real clue as to how they are going to move forward. The reality of the matter is that if you haven't even done research on the local market then you won't actually know if the price you paid was a steal or if you were taken advantage of. When considering property investments, it is always important to remember that just because a given property is a good deal, doesn't mean it is a good deal for you, right now. With early real estate investment deals you have too much on the line to do yourself the disservice of moving forward with a property before having an airtight course of action ready to go. Pricing out properties is discussed in more detail in chapters 5 and 6.

Not keeping your expectations in check: While some properties can quickly and easily be turned around for a substantial profit, these are the exception, not the rule. In order to meet the strict 18-month deadline, you are going to need to start with properties that need a lot of work, which means having a realistic timeframe for just how long everything is going to take, and thus when you can expect to see a profit, is crucial when it comes to ensuring that you will be prepared both mentally and financially for the tribulations to come. To understand the average timeframe, consider the following regarding just what a successful real estate investment entails.

First you will need to do the research on the area you are considering investing in as well as researching numerous different options before finding one that meets your needs. Then, once you make an offer, you can expect to wait for upwards of three months if you have gone ahead and gotten preapproval through a traditional bank. Even if everything is aces, you will still likely need to factor in about a month before your name is on the deed.

Selling a property can be a process that moves quickly from the very first open house. Unfortunately, it can also drag on insufferably, largely based on factors that are outside of your control. While the stars can align and random chance can work in your favor, the odds that somewhere along the process something is going to go wrong are too high not to factor into the process. Speed is not one of real estate's investing's virtues but what it lacks in quick turnaround times it makes up for in reliability.

Thinking you can do it all yourself: While having faith in yourself is an admirable quality, when it comes to real estate investment odds are not only will you not be able to do it all yourself, you are almost certainly not going to want to, especially if you want to hit that 18-month window. While some people will have all the skills required to complete a house full of renovations all by themselves, the time that this will take will almost always mean that this is a poor value proposition at best. You are going to want to complete between two and three complete flips in an 18-month window and that is not something anyone can realistically expect to do on their own.

Real estate investment is a numbers game which means that you will always see greater overall returns by taking a smaller personal cut of each property and working quickly and efficiently with a team than trying to make as much profit as possible and doing it all yourself. At the very least, you are going to need a real estate investment lawyer, a CPA and a reliable contractor. The specifics on building a team are discussed in the next chapter.

The importance of nurturing these relationships once you have them cannot be over-stressed. They will quite often be the difference between success and failure. You will be working with these individuals on a regular basis and you will need their help to generate the type of active or passive income stream that you are looking for. Go out of you want to build trust and form bonds beyond the realm of the traditional service person/customer relationship. While the extra work might seem pointless at first, the results will more than pay for themselves with time.

Never getting the best deals possible: While you won't be able to take every negotiation to the point where you are getting your ideal price every single time, it is important to not let things get to the point where you are routinely giving up more than you should just to close a deal. These concessions, while seemingly minor, can easily add up over time, pushing your goal of $100,000 per year back in the process. When going into every negotiation, you are going to need to know what your ideal number is going to be, the maximum amount you can give up and still make the minimum profit you need to move forward with the project and the number where you are simply going to want to walk away because the deal is no longer profitable.

Additionally, you are going to want to stick to this philosophy regardless if you are putting down money on a new property or simply buying a box of nails from the hardware store. While these smaller numbers might not seem like much individually, they too will add up overtime and account for a significant drain on your profits if left unchecked. Be sure not to let a lax attitude affect your bottom line, always be aware of the true cost of any concessions you make.

Not knowing what you're signing: Another problem that many new real estate investors run into is after they go to the trouble of doing their research, make a plan based around a specific property, then then rush through the loan acquisition process without making sure they understand the finer points of the contract they end up signing. Not having a clear understanding of these finer points is akin to gambling with your long-term investment, a poor choice no matter what situation you find yourself in. Failing to understand the specifics of your loan agreement can easily lead you to paying thousands more than you were anticipating based on inaccurate assumptions alone.

Lowballing renovation costs: Early on you may find that it is difficult for you to accurately determine the cost for the specific renovations a property might need as you have never had to do so before. Underestimating these costs can be dangerous, however, as it can end up leaving you in a position where you have committed all your available resources to a project and still come up short. This is why you will always be better off overestimating these costs while also factoring in the maintenance fees that will be required while you are trying to get the property sold. Don't forget the insurance and taxes as well. Over time, when working with a contractor, you should get a feel for what these sorts of things typically cost.

Treating investments causally: Just because investing in real estate is often thought of as a long-term investment doesn't mean that you can afford to approach it casually, especially if you hope to start seeing serious results in just 18 months. Your real estate investments are a business and should be treated as such. Only by showing real dedication and true commitment will you ever realistically see a reliable return; when it comes to investments you will only ever get back from them what you put in multiplied by the amount of effort you put forth.

Chapter 4: Getting Started with Your 18-month Strategy

The basic outline of the 18-month strategy to help you to earn $100,000 per year revolves around finding ugly duckling properties, polishing them until they shine and then selling them for a significant profit. If you can do this just three or four times over the course of the first 18 months then you will have netted your first $100,000 and be on your way to setting up a system whereby you can safely assume the money will keep rolling in. Once you reach that point. you will then want to slowly start shifting from fixing and flipping properties to fixing and holding them to rent out in order to ensure a passive income stream that will last you for the rest of your life. The details for doing both can be found in the next two chapters.

Ugly duckling properties: An ugly duckling property is simply a property that most people would not think of looking at twice simply because it needs a bit of extra work. The more extra work required, the greater the potential for profit once you have fixed it up and found its inner beauty.

While the potential for profit with ugly duckling properties is going to be higher than with properties that are more or less ready to resell right away, the risk is also going to be higher as well. Ugly duckling properties can have any number of unexpected surprises attached which can turn an otherwise stellar investment into an unmitigated nightmare. This means you are always going to want to have a backup plan in case the original plan for the property doesn't pan out like you hoped. At the very least, you need to consider that the property may very will sit unsold and vacant for a prolonged period of time.

Investing in ugly duckling properties, and thus following this 18-month plan, isn't going to be right for everyone. It has proven to be the correct investment choice for those who like to be directly in charge of their own investments, like the idea of being able to hold their investments in their hands, and even walk around inside them, and enjoy finding a great deal even if it takes a little extra work.

The key to finding good ugly duckling properties is the ability to see past whatever it is that is causing the property in question to be seen as an ugly duckling and see the potential for risk and reward instead. This means you will need to be able to determine what the likely renovation costs are going to be, or pay someone to do it for you, and then determine if the overall potential for profit is going to be worth the price of admission.

Finding the right properties
In order to take your first steps to making the 18-month plan a reality, the first thing you are going to need to do is to find the right properties. To find the types of properties you are looking for, you are going to want to forgo the typical channels and go where the real potential for profit lives.

Motivated sellers: One of the best ways to find property that lots of investors aren't already fighting over is to find sellers before they make it into the system. Once a seller has a real estate agent, the odds of getting the best possible price decreases dramatically. This means you are going to want to reach out to sellers before they realize they want to sell. The best candidate for this process is what is known as a motivated seller. These are individuals who have pressing financial needs that need to be cleared up ASAP. You then have the ability to step in with an offer that can make the issue go away and everyone (but mostly you) wins.

While it may sound surprising, the best way to find motivated sellers is through a direct marketing campaign. Assuming you live in at least a city of a medium size, you should be able to find a local company that will sell you a list of people who are currently sitting on a sizeable pile of debt for a few hundred dollars. With these details in hand, you simply do a little digging at the County Clerk's office and cross off everyone who doesn't currently own their home.

Once you have a list of potential sellers you then simply draft a form letter outlining the fact that you have found out (don't say how) that they are in financial trouble and explain that you are offering a solution, in cash. Make sure to express regret at their hardship as well and indicate that you are on their side. You don't want to make an offer in the letter, however, but instead express interest in getting together and discussing the situation in detail.

While every letter won't lead to success, out of about 300 possible hits you will likely come back with around 10 individuals who are interested in what you have to say which should be enough to get you started. From there it is simply a matter of assessing the value of the property compared to what the individual owes and then lowballing them enough to ensure that you can still make a sizeable profit even after repairs and renovations have been completed.

Find a team
Regardless of how handy you feel you are, it is virtually impossible to make it through an entire renovation by yourself, especially in a timeframe that will gel with the 18-month plan. As such, it is important to go out of your way to establish a strong team to help you out early on, as doing so will pay dividends for years to come, even after the costs of using them are taken into account.

The first person you are going to want to hire is a real estate lawyer and a certified public accountant that specializes in handling real estate investments. While you will hopefully never have to make serious use of these individuals, having them in your pocket will make any situations where you do imminently more manageable. These services are going to be costly, though the fees are not regulated which means you will be able to shop around or negotiate a price, just be sure not to sacrifice quality in service of saving a few dollars.

Next you will want to find a good real estate agent who will be able to help you sell the properties as quickly as possible once they are ready to go. While you can skip this recommendation, and set up your own open houses and advertising, your goal should be to turn around the property as quickly as possible and a good real estate agent will be worth their commission if they can do this reliably. They will also have access to channels that you don't and will sometimes be able to help you find properties as well. A good working relationship with a real estate agent can truly help you take your real estate investing to the next level.

General contractor: A reliable general contractor is worth their weight in gold. This person will be in charge of the day to day work on your investment property and will ideally come with their own crew as well which means you won't need to go out of you way to hire a dozen different specialists. While finding the right contractor can be time consuming, it will be time well spent if you follow through on it properly. The best way to find a good contractor is to start by getting recommendations, ideally from a local real estate investment club or from someone else who has reason to know what they are talking about. Barring that, you can visit local lumber mills and ask them for the names of the contractors who always use the highest quality materials as that is typically a sign of good work all-around.

You will then want to take your list and meet with the contractors face to face. In person interviews are crucial as you will, in theory, be working with one of these individuals on a regular basis which means it is important that you get along on a personal as well as a professional level. During the interviews, you are going to want to find out what types of projects they are comfortable handling, references, what type of team they bring to the table and the number of jobs they typically take on at once. Ideally you will want to end up with a primary contractor and a backup contractor to ensure you can start any new job before the ink has fully dried on the contract.

Chapter 5: Flipping Properties

Flipping ugly duckling properties is the key to making $100,000 in 18-months and then using those profits to generate a steady return of $100,000 per year from your investments. In order to do so reliably you are going to want to have a team in place and already have done the required research when it comes to finding good deals.

Fundamentals
ARV: The most important number when it comes to any potential property is the After Repair Value (ARV). ARV is the amount you will be able to plan on selling the home for one everything about it has been improved to the point of show condition. You will always want to underestimate the ARV due to the fact that overestimation can easily lead to a significant decrease in the profits you make once everything is said and done.

In order to determine the ARV, you are going to want to take the amount you can get the property for and add to it the amount it will cost to fix it up along with any fees you may be paying for use of the money you are using to do so. The end result should be less than 70 percent of what you plan to make on the property and that number should equal between $25,000 and $30,000 depending on the amount of work that needs to be done to the property as you will need to do between three and four successful flips to hit your goal. If the property doesn't hit these numbers then you will want to move on as there are better choices out there.

It is important to have a clear understanding of what the ARV is likely to be when you go an visit the property for the first time as this will ensure that you won't have to worry about your emotions getting in the way of making the right decision or having to determine the ARV after the fact. While sticking to this rule might seem unnecessarily strict, shifting even 5 percent away from it can lead to significant losses, especially if issues arise that you didn't foresee.

Understand the likely buyers: When it comes to setting the right ARV, it is important to also understand who you are going to be targeting as your buyers when everything is said and done. This will ensure you can accurately determine the quality of the overall remodel as well as what you will be able to sell the property for. If you are looking at properties in rural areas then you will want to ensure there is plenty of room for animals and ancillary vehicles, as well as fewer government restrictions. On the other hand, areas with good school and family-friendly amenities are going to attract families which means you are going to want to prioritize yard space and extra bathrooms.

There is money to be made from all different types of properties, regardless of the layout, as long as you have a clear idea of who you are creating the home for. Play to the strengths of the property and you will not only save on remodeling costs, you will find that selling the property is easier in the long run as well.

Understand the value you create: As you make improvements to a property, it is important to keep a running tally of the value you are adding to it. Likewise, it is important to take plenty of before pictures to show to potential buyers so they can see how much the property has improved which helps to justify your asking price. This is not to say that you need to completely gut every property completely and more or less start from scratch, it is important to never begin an improvement if it is going to cost more than the amount of value it adds to the final selling price.

While you aren't going to want to leave things in a faulty or unsafe condition, you are also going to want to think twice before doing things like renovating a living room that is a little smaller than average. Your bottom line should always be in the front of your mind when you are making a list of changes your team needs to implement.

When it comes to things such as decorating and painting, you are always going to want to stick with neutral colors, not plain white, and go with generic decisions whenever possible. Whatever you do, you want it to be as easy as possible for a wide variety of people to be able to move in and transplant their style with ease. Everyone who sees the completed property should be able to immediately see themselves living there and an aggressive color or style choice is only going to appeal to a limited portion of the population.

Two things that you are always going to want to update are going to be the fixtures in the kitchen and those in the bathroom. A small change in these spaces can go a long way towards making older homes feel fresh while only adding a small cost to your bottom line. This includes things like light switch covers, mirrors and faucets. While a new toilet and shower can quickly send costs spiraling to epic heights, a $120 sink can easily change the entire feel of a bathroom.

In the kitchen, you are also always going to want to modernize the cabinet doors as this will change the feel of the whole space dramatically. If they are in good working order, the refrigerator and the oven can be left as they are, as long as they are clean enough to be mistaken as new. Skipping this step can leave a perceived layer of grime throughout the space that hurts your sale's chances time and again. As such, you should always hire a professional cleaning service prior to showing the house no matter what.

Don't get too attached: While it is important to do everything in your power in order to ensure that a property is going to look as good as possible, at the same time you are going to want to everything in your power to ensure that you remain relatively divorced from the proceedings so you can keep a critical eye on things as they progress. If you aren't careful, it is very easy to find yourself growing attached to the property and letting your emotions influence the price you think it is worth. This is always going to be a folly however, as the only things that should alter the ARV of the property once you have purchased it are the market value in the area and the strength of the market overall. Don't forget, you shouldn't be striving for the maximum price possible, you should be prioritizing speed of sale. The faster you manage to sell the property, the faster you will be able to get down to getting business finding another to repeat the process with.

Keeping costs down

Break tasks down to component parts: While staring at everything that needs to be done to a property is enough to give most people a panic attack, it helps to break tasks down into their component parts. Not only will this make it easier to cope with what needs to be accomplished, you will also save money because you will be able to determine what is required for each job up front which means you are more likely to get a bulk discount. You will want to go room by room and make a list of what needs to be done so you can be sure you don't miss anything, and also show that list to potential buyers when the time comes to sell.

Nurture supplier relationships: When you are first getting started flipping properties you are going to want to do additional legwork up front so that you can count on getting better prices in the long-term on products you know you are going to be buying in bulk time and again. Keep in mind that running to the store and buying parts last minute is going to be a serious drain on your profits if it is not kept in check.

Instead, purchasing products in bulk from a local supplier will not only allow you to establish the price for things more accurately at the start, it will lead to additional savings if done appropriately. To get started, all you need to do is ask to speak to the manager at the local hardware or construction supply store. The best bet in these cases is to find a local business instead of a chain as they will likely be more willing and able to make a deal.

After you find the right person to talk to, you will want to show them your list of products and let them know that you are going to be in the renovation business for a long time and that you are looking to establish mutually beneficial relationships now, to save yourself time later. Once it is clear what you are offering, all you need to do is to ask what type of discount they might be able to provide on your bulk orders in exchange for assurances that you will be doing all of your business at their store for the foreseeable future. While this won't work every time, it shouldn't take you more than a few stops to find someone who is willing to make a deal.

Always be on the lookout for deals: In addition to buying in bulk, you are going to want to get into the habit of keeping an eye out for good deals on products that could be potentially useful in future renovations and stock up while the price is right. One particular area that it is frequently worth keeping an eye out for deals is when it comes to granite for smaller countertops. A granite countertop will add a good deal of class to a master bathroom, but the costs on fresh granite can be quite steep. As such, you can keep an eye out for pieces of granite that have major flaws in the middle, and then have your team cut them yourselves and pick them up for sometimes as much as 20 percent of the regular price.

Chapter 6: Rental Properties

Once you have successfully made your first $100,000, you will want to start looking at relevant properties with a different eye. While you will want to ensure that you are flipping enough houses to ensure that your extra income remains stable, you will also want to start picking properties to hold on to. Rental properties are a great long-term investment strategy that can generate a significant amount of monthly revenue, especially if you pick them up on the cheap as ugly-duckling properties to start with, and have most, if not all, of the asking price ready to go up front.

Rental renovation tips
While most of what passed for reliable advice in the previous chapter will still apply, there are a few additional factors you are going to want to keep in mind when it comes to renovating properties for rent as opposed to sale.

Cut costs in the right places: While it will still be extremely important to do all that you can in order to get rid of the ugly duckling vibe from the property in order to promote rentability, renters aren't buyers which means that you don't need to do as much to ensure the property is perfect. A good rule of thumb with rental properties is that you are going to want to focus on the areas that will make the property easier to rent out. This means you are going to want to stick to basic livability changes in the bedrooms and then focus on the bathrooms and kitchen, including fixtures, countertops and cabinets which means you can typically do both rooms for about $1,000 total.

Look for good prices, not cheap materials: While you might be tempted to go with the cheapest options available when it comes to rental properties, you need to make sure that you aren't going to end up actually costing yourself more in the long run. Cheaper products tend to wear out more quickly, typically twice as fast, than products that are as little as 20 percent more expensive which means you are going to have to replace them year after year. It is typically better to get the majority of your costs out of the way upfront as opposed to replacing cheap products on a regular basis.

Rental property math
Property management: If you are interested in managing the property yourself, you are likely going to be in a better position to do so than most, simply because you already have a contractor you can call when it comes to doing repairs on the property and a list of suppliers who can give you a good deal on parts. However, if you are interested in generating passive income from your rental properties then you will want to look into a property management company. Property management companies will deal with tenants directly so you don't have to, which is a big plus for many landlords.

When it comes to using property management companies, it is important to do your research regarding which one makes the most since for you. The average cost of one of these companies is between 8 and 12 percent of the monthly rental price. When you are first starting out you will likely need to add as much as an extra 10 percent on top of this costs as very few property management companies are going to be interested in working with a single, single family home. While these fees will eventually drop as you find more properties to rent out, this is likely what you can expect to pay from the start.

Pricing your rental: You should already have a general idea of what you are planning to charge for the property based on the ARV and the rates of similar rental properties in the area. From there you will want to consider any marketable extras you have added to the property as well as anything about it that makes it unique for the market. The goal here should be to ensure you aren't shortchanging yourself while also not overestimating the work that has been done, remember, the more expensive the property the greater the likelihood that it is going to sit empty prior to finding a renter.

If you are having trouble determining what to charge for the property, you will want to first consider what tier the property falls into now that it has been fixed up. The highest tier of property is going to be those that are likely going to attract the best tenants possible and it is unlikely you will ever have trouble finding tenants who will pay top dollar for the privilege of living there. Very few ugly duckling properties are going to reach this tier. Second tier properties are the most common types of rentals that you see, they are not the pick of the litter but they are well-constructed homes in average or better neighborhoods, not flashy but not shabby either. When fixing up an ugly duckling property you will want to shoot for this tier.

For tier two properties the overall risk of vacancy is still going to be relatively low, and if there is a vacancy it is unlikely to last more than a month. As you likely got the property for a great deal, you are going to want to strive to get back 2 percent of your total investment per month in rent which means the property will be purely making money in just about five years. As such, if you paid $100,000 for the property and the renovations then you would want to charge $2,000 per month to see a reasonable return on your investment eventually.

If you end up with a third-tier property, either because the renovations didn't work out as smoothly as you hoped or if the neighbor is on the rougher side then you are going to need to charge more for rent to balance out the additional risks associated with the investment. These properties will likely sit empty for two months or more between tenants and you will want to be less strict when it comes to choosing tenants as they are unlikely to stick around for more than the length of their lease anyway. You will want to aim for 3 percent of your investment per month with these properties for the best results.

In addition to what you will be making in rent, when it comes to determining what your long-term profits will be you are going to need to factor in the average 3 percent that most properties appreciate by per year. Unfortunately, you are also going to need to subtract out fees associated with maintenance costs, property management fees, repairs, taxes, insurance and months where the property sits vacant. Furthermore, you may find it a helpful exercise to assume that a full 50 percent of your yearly profits are going to be squandered by major repairs or by responding to other types of emergencies. While this won't always be the case, when the repairs are required they are likely to be quite expensive so it should all balance out in the end.

While this might not leave much coming in as pure profit per month, you will need to think about the property in terms of its long-term value instead. You never know when the market is going to experience a huge jump in your favor and it will suddenly make more sense to sell off the property and take advantage of the market scarcity to make a huge profit. Regardless, you are likely going to be seeing greater than the average 7 return on investment that many investments see, and the volatility for housing investments is practically non-existent. With enough investment properties, you won't even need to complete fix and flips anymore.

Advertising
Once you are ready to rent out a property it is important to do everything you can to ensure the vacancy is filled as quickly as possible. The day after renovations are completed is the day the property starts costing you money while it is sitting vacant. When it comes to getting the most effective advertising for a new rental property for the cheapest price, the best place to start is with social media.

You are going to want to start the social media campaign for the property on the day that you start the renovations. Taking pictures of the property throughout the process will serve as a timeline showing how much value has been added to it through the work you have done. Having digital proof of these things will help to ease the minds of potential renters as they won't simply have to take your word that specific repairs were done.

What's more, studies show that each person is never more than three degrees of separation from someone that is in the market for a new place to live at least 50 percent of the time which means that making sure your property gets in front of as many eyes as possible is a great way to find prospective tenants. If you can spread the word to just twenty people outside of your personal social circle then you are quite likely to find a renter without even having to worry about posting a for rent sign in the front yard.

Screening tenants

Once you have found some prospective tenants, the next thing you will need to do is find the most reliable one to start paying you rent without destroying all the value you have already added to the property. The first thing you are going to need to do to get this process underway is understand the landlord laws in your area to make sure that you are exercising your rights as fully as possible while at the same time not infringing on the rights of your future tenants.

The screening policy that is right for you is going to be as unique as your overall investment plan, simply because different things are going to be right for different landlords. Some will feel the need to exacting in their tenant selection process and others will feel comfortable knowing just the basics of who they are renting to. While the right approach for you is likely somewhere in the middle of these extremes, what a lot of it is going to come down to is what level of risk you feel is acceptable. If you are too strict then you run the risk of turning away potentially viable tenants and if you are too lenient then you run the risk of losing value on your property. Regardless of where you fall on the spectrum, you are going to want to keep a few crucial considerations in mind.

First and foremost, you are going to want to ensure that they haven't had any evictions within the last ten years. While a lot can happen in ten years and going back to far can punish responsible adults for youthful transactions, this is enough time to protect you from serial renters who move from place to place, staying only long enough to be evicted. For your first rental property a firm stance of no evictions, period, is perfectly acceptable.

You will also want to look at references from employers and previous landlords, even if you don't use them. Having tenants who are confident enough to put down this information is typically a strong enough sign that they expect the results to be positive. If you do follow up, as a potential landlord you have the right to ask basic relevant questions, just be sure not to pry unduly.

A background check should be a non-negotiable part of your screening process. Felonies that include violent crimes and dangerous drugs should be enough to disqualify potential tenants under most circumstances, though you may want to give the felon the chance to explain what happened. Keeping things simple and avoiding anyone with a felony in the past 10 years is often enough to weed out the riff-raff.

When it comes to determining the right level of income for your new tenant(s), it is important to ensure that they are always going to be able to pay the rent no matter what. As such, an income total of all relevant parties that is at least three times the total of the rent should be enough to prevent you from holding the bag should times get tough.

If your screening turns up things that you like, it is important to always send out a rejection letter to the would-be tenant. This is known as an adverse actions letter and it will let them know what actions you took as part of the screening process, what the results you revealed and why you made the decision you did. You will need to send this out within sixty days of when the screening was completed to comply with federal law.

Conclusion

Thank you for making it through to the end of *Property Investing: How to Create Wealth and Passive Income Through Smart Buy & Hold Real Estate Investing. An Exact 18-Month Strategy for Making an Extra 100k Per Year*, let's hope it was informative and able to provide you with all of the tools you need to achieve your goals in just 18 months.

The next step is to stop reading about real estate investment and to get your boots on the ground and start making it a reality for you. The only way to be successful with this plan is to dedicate the next year and a half to it, come hell or high water. Remember, while it may seem as though the odds are stacked against you, as long as you persevere you really can make your dreams a reality.

Finally, if you found this book useful in anyway, a review on Amazon is always appreciated!

Description

If you are interested in leaving the 9-to-5 world behind and instead being your own boss while still making six figures per year, then *Property Investing: How to Create Wealth and Passive Income Through Smart Buy & Hold Real Estate Investing. An Exact 18-Month Strategy for Making an Extra 100k Per Year* is the book you have been waiting for.

Real estate investment is one of the oldest and most reliable forms of investment in the world and if you follow the plan outlined inside you can start seeing real results in just a year and a half. While it might sound too good to be true, this is no get rich quick scheme, it is simply an accelerated way of taking advantage of the real estate market, the same way that Warren Buffet, Donald Trump and countless others have done for generations. All it takes is hard work, determination, and a little luck, and before you know it you will not only be generating a six-figure income, you will be on your way to building long-term passive income as well.

So, what are you waiting for? Stop waiting for your ship to come in and grab the bull by the horns. Take control of your financial future and buy this book today!

Inside you will find
- How to train your brain to be ready for true financial success through a property investment mindset.
- Surefire ways of funding your first real estate investment with as little as no money down.
- The easiest way of finding sellers who are just waiting for you to take their home off their hands.
- One simple trick for ensuring that you never overpay for a property investment.
- The easiest way to find rental properties that are sure to turn a profit
- ***And more...***

www.ingramcontent.com/pod-product-compliance
Lightning Source LLC
Chambersburg PA
CBHW050016230526
45470CB00003B/993